High-Tech DIY Projects with Flying Objects

Maggie Murphy

New York

Published in 2015 by The Rosen Publishing Group, Inc.
29 East 21st Street, New York, NY 10010

First Edition

Editors: Jennifer Way and Jacob Seifert
Book Design: Andrew Povolny
Photo Research: Katie Stryker

Photo Credits: Cover Thomas J. Abercrombie/NATIONAL GEOGRAPHIC IMAGE COLLECTION/Getty Images; p. 4 DEA PICTURE LIBRARY/De Agostini/Getty Images; p. 5 National Archives/Hulton Archive/Getty Images; pp. 6, 9 (bottom) Hulton Archive/Getty Images; p. 7 Stock Montage/Archive Photos/Getty Images; p. 9 (top) Geoff Dann /Dorling Kindersley/Getty Images; p. 10 Purestock/Thinkstock; p. 11 Raul Touzon/NATIONAL GEOGRAPHIC IMAGE COLLECTION/Getty Images; p. 12 Stephen Hardy/iStock/Thinkstock; p. 13 George Marks/Retrofile RF /Getty Images; pp. 14, 20 Education Images/Universal Images Group/Getty Images; p. 15 Paul Bradbury /Caiaimage/Getty Images; pp. 16–19, 23–25 Katie Stryker; p. 21 Miami Herald/McClatchy-Tribune/Getty Images; p. 26 Sven Hagolani/Getty Images; p. 27 Elenarts/iStock/Thinkstock; p. 28 Pete Pahham /Shutterstock.com; p. 29 (top) Peter Barrett/iStock/Thinkstock; p. 29 (bottom) Grégory DUBUS/iStock/Thinkstock. Project Credit: pp. 16–18 courtesy of Braedon O'Meara.

Library of Congress Cataloging-in-Publication Data

Murphy, Maggie, author.
High-tech DIY projects with flying objects / by Maggie Murphy. — First edition.
    pages cm. — (Maker kids)
Includes index.
ISBN 978-1-4777-6673-6 (library binding) — ISBN 978-1-4777-6679-8 (pbk.) —
ISBN 978-1-4777-6660-6 (6-pack)
1. Rockets (Aeronautics)—Models—Design and construction—Juvenile literature. 2. Catapults (Aeronautics)—Design and construction—Juvenile literature. I. Title. II. Title: High-tech do-it-yourself projects with flying objects.
TL547.M85 2015
621.43'56022'8—dc23
                    2014003217

Manufactured in the United States of America

CPSIA Compliance Information: Batch #WS14PK9: For Further Information contact Rosen Publishing, New York, New York at 1-800-237-9932

Contents

Making Objects Fly

Throughout history, people have been interested in flight. Insects, birds, and flying mammals have inspired many people to build flying objects. Ancient peoples used **catapults** to throw big, heavy rocks through the air. In the 1950s, many countries raced to launch rockets and send **satellites**, which are machines that gather information, into space. Today, kids like you are building their own high-tech flying objects for fun!

People have tried to make flying machines for centuries. Italian scientist and artist Leonardo da Vinci drew this image of a flying machine around 1505.

The Wright brothers completed the first successful aircraft flight in Kitty Hawk, North Carolina, in 1903.

The maker movement is all about experimenting with do-it-yourself (DIY) projects. In this book, you will learn how to build flying objects by following step-by-step instructions. As you make these projects, you'll also learn about the science that makes them work!

All About Catapults

One of the earliest machines invented for making objects fly through the air is the catapult. The catapult was first invented around 400 BC and used by the Greeks and Romans during war. Catapults were often used to **propel** heavy objects, such as boulders, into walls and towers or at enemy soldiers.

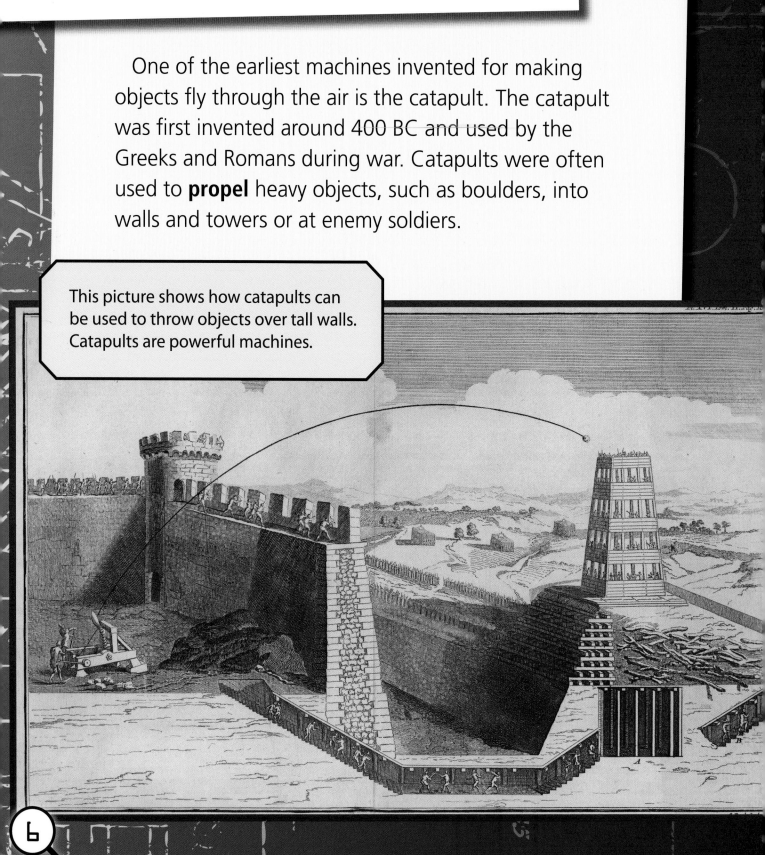

This picture shows how catapults can be used to throw objects over tall walls. Catapults are powerful machines.

Some catapults are loaded by pulling or cranking back the arms. When the arm is released, it shoots forward and sends the loaded object flying.

Catapults don't only throw big rocks, though. **Medieval** people loaded catapults with garbage, things they set on fire, and even corpses to send over tall castle walls. During World War I, armies used catapults to launch grenades at their enemies. Special catapults, called aircraft catapults, have even been used to help get planes into the air.

There are different kinds of catapults, but all catapults are made with a kind of simple machine called a lever. A lever is a strong surface that pivots on a fixed point called a **fulcrum**. Levers are good for moving things, called loads. When effort is applied to a lever, it moves on its fulcrum and this moves the load.

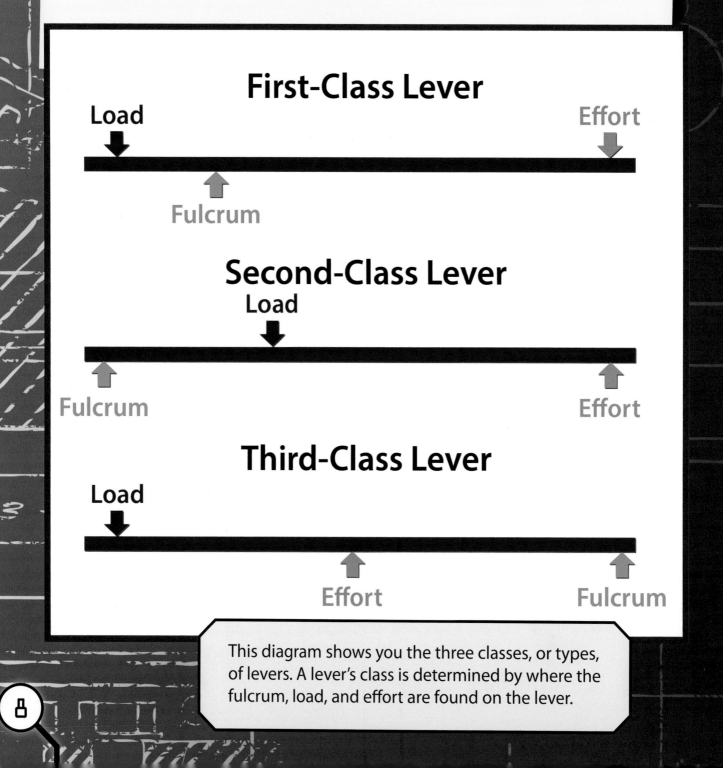

First-Class Lever

Load   Effort

Fulcrum

Second-Class Lever

Load

Fulcrum   Effort

Third-Class Lever

Load

Effort   Fulcrum

This diagram shows you the three classes, or types, of levers. A lever's class is determined by where the fulcrum, load, and effort are found on the lever.

Fulcrum

There are three classes of levers, called first class, second class, and third class. A lever's class is determined by where the fulcrum is in relation to the load and effort. Since there are several kinds of catapults, not all catapults are the same kind of lever. On a catapult, the fulcrum is where the arm connects to the frame, the load is what is being thrown from the catapult, and the effort is whatever moves the arm.

Effort

The mangonel is a catapult that is a third-class lever because the effort is applied between the load and fulcrum.

Fulcrum

Load

Effort

How Do Rockets Work?

Rockets are long, thin objects that shoot through water, air, or outer space. They have special kinds of **engines** called rocket engines. Missiles and spaceships are examples of rockets.

A rocket engine uses a type of **fuel** that has small amounts of oxygen in it. This lets rocket engines burn in outer space, where there is no air. Some rocket engines burn solid fuel, while others use liquid fuel.

This is the space shuttle *Atlantis*. The big reddish part holds fuel that is needed for blastoff. It will come off once the fuel has been used.

This kind of rocket engine was used on *Saturn V* rockets. NASA used *Saturn V* rockets to send humans to the Moon.

When the fuel burns, it turns into hot gas. The engine pushes the gas out the back. This pushes the rocket in whatever direction it is pointing. When a rocket is on the ground and pointed toward the sky, the rocket will shoot up.

Ground Rats

Gunpowder was invented in China over 2,000 years ago. About 900 years ago, Chinese inventors experimented with filling bamboo tubes with gunpowder. The English term for what the Chinese called these is ground rats. When lit, a ground rat would fly around the ground, hit something, and then go in a new direction. This was the beginning of rocket science.

Model Rockets

Model rockets can be launched a few different ways. One popular way is to use a solid-fuel engine.

When using a solid-fuel engine, a model rocket will need a launch system. This launch system is made up of a launchpad, an **igniter**, long electrical wires, and a handheld launcher. This allows you to stay safe and stand far back from your rocket as you launch it.

Safety is important when launching a model rocket. Always stand far away from the rocket when you ignite it.

Model rockets were created in the 1950s. Making them quickly became a hobby that many people enjoyed. Many people still enjoy making model rockets today.

You can buy a solid-fuel engine by itself or in a kit that also has everything else you will need to make a model rocket. Make sure always to have an adult there to help you with your rocket engine.

3D Print Your Rocket

There are many ways to make a rocket. One new way is to 3D print some of the parts. There is a tutorial, downloadable files, and instructions at Instructables.com/id/3D-Print-flying -model-rockets that will tell you everything you need to know. Just design your rocket pieces using a special computer program and then use a 3D printer to print them. Put together the rocket using those printed pieces and other parts that you can't 3D print, such as a parachute and fuel. Then all that's left to do is blast off!

Join a Club!

If you like the idea of building flying objects with other kids, you might want to join a club! A club is a group made up of members who share an interest. Your school or local library may have a science club, rocket club, or robotics club for you to join. There, you can learn about the science behind flying objects, share your ideas, and work with others to build cool projects.

In some rocket-making clubs, members see who can build the rocket that goes the highest. This helps the club members experiment, learn, and have fun.

The list at Pbskids.org/scigirls/find-a-science-club has tons of clubs for girls who want to get into rocketry, science, and more.

The Internet is a great place to find out if there is a rocket club near you. Ask an adult to help you look for one at Flyrockets.com/clubs_db.asp. If there are no nearby clubs to join, ask a teacher or librarian about starting one.

Make a Catapult

Catapults may not be what we think of as high-tech today, but they were at the cutting edge of technology when they were invented. Follow the instructions in this chapter to make a catapult with just a few household items.

You will need to have an adult help you with the wire cutters and hot-glue gun. Be careful not to poke yourself when bending the paper clips and pushing in the pushpins.

You will need:

- 2 large paper clips
- 2 pushpins
- Ballpoint pen casing (ink removed)
- Plastic bottle cap
- Scotch tape
- Pair of wire cutters
- Paper or tinfoil to make balls
- Hot-glue gun and hot-glue sticks

Place the paper clips flat on the table and bend the outside legs out slightly. Bend the inner folded parts up.

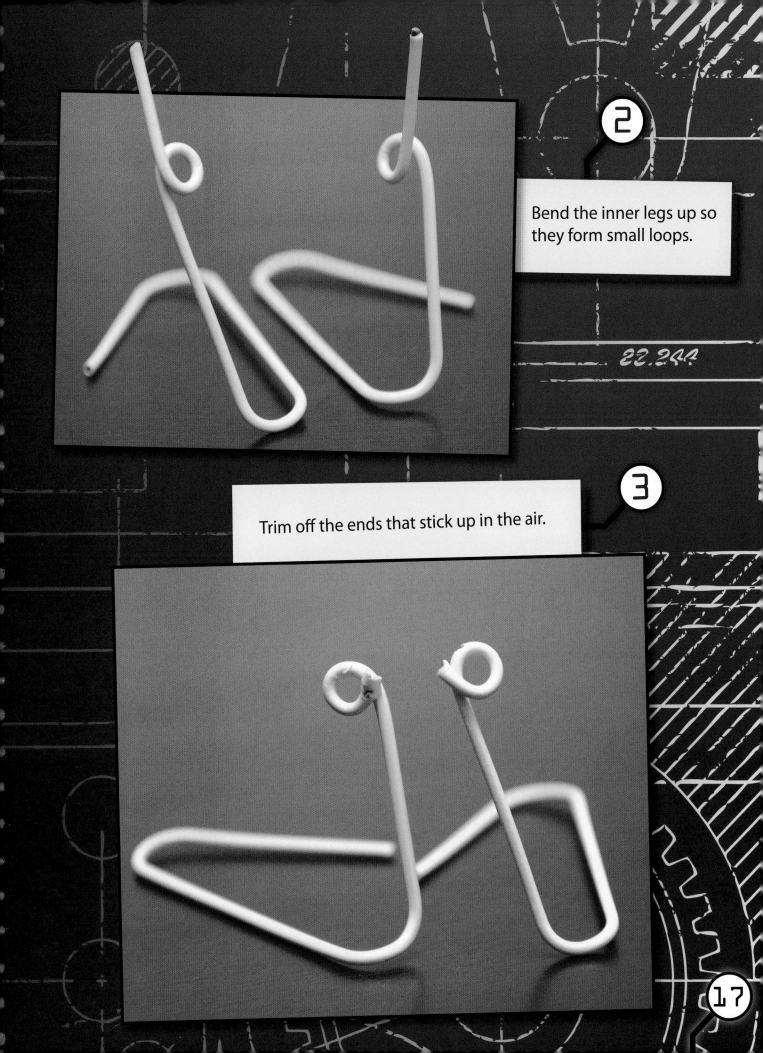

Bend the inner legs up so they form small loops.

Trim off the ends that stick up in the air.

Hold the pen casing between the two paper clip loops about a third of the way down the length of the pen. Push a pin through each loop into the pen.

Put a couple pieces of tape across the top and bottom of the paper clip base. This will keep the legs from moving.

Use the hot-glue gun to secure the bottle cap to the end of the pen farthest from the pushpins.

22.244

Your catapult is now ready to fire! Put a ball of paper or tinfoil in the plastic bottle cap, hold down the base with one finger, and slam down the short end with another finger.

10

25

50

Make a target for yourself out of paper. You can fire your catapult at it to see how good of a shot you are.

Rocket Projects

You can find many rocket projects on Instructables.com. Instructables.com is a website with thousands of fun DIY projects for you to try. Each project includes a list of materials needed to build your launcher and rocket. Many rocket-building materials can be purchased at local hardware or hobby stores. You can also buy a model rocket kit online from websites such as Estesrockets.com, Makershed.com, and Amazon.com.

You may want to launch a premade model rocket before you build your own. This way, you can see how rockets are supposed to fly.

There are plenty of high-tech rocket kits you can buy. They come with everything you need so you don't have to track everything down.

Safety First

You will need an adult to help you build most rocket projects. Some projects require tools such as drills and handsaws. Some rockets are launched with combustible fuel, which can be very dangerous if it is not used correctly. You can read about safety tips for launching model rockets with fuel engines at Exploration.grc.nasa.gov /education/rocket /rktsafe.html.

As you look through projects, you will find that there are many different kinds of rockets you can build. One of the most fun kinds is a water rocket. The next chapter will teach you how to build one.

Make a Water Rocket

You must have an adult help you with this project. Have an adult use the power drill, lighter, scissors, matches or lighter, and PVC primer and cement so you don't hurt yourself.

You will need to clean your PVC pipes before you start the project. Make sure to use PVC primer on the ends that you will connect. Because the PVC cement has strong fumes, do this project outside or in a room with good ventilation. When you shoot off your rocket, do it in a large open area so it doesn't hit someone or something when it lands.

You will need:

- 60-inch (152 cm) length of .5-inch (1 cm) PVC pipe
- 12-inch (30 cm) length of .5-inch (1 cm) PVC pipe
- 3-inch (8 cm) length of .5-inch (1 cm) PVC pipe
- 2-inch (5 cm) length of 1.5-inch (4 cm) PVC pipe
- Two .5-inch (1 cm) PVC end caps
- .5-inch (1 cm) PVC tee
- PVC primer
- PVC pipe cement
- Clamp for 1.5-inch (4 cm) hose
- Replacement valve for a tubeless tire
- Plastic cable ties
- Candle
- Matches or lighter
- Two 2-liter soda bottles
- Twine or nylon string
- Power drill with .5-inch (1 cm) bit
- Scissors
- Bicycle tire pump
- Duct tape
- Marker

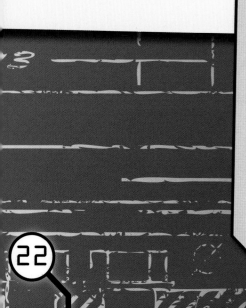

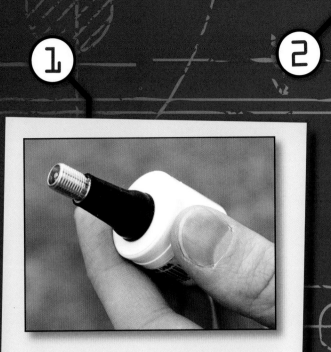

Drill a hole through one of the PVC caps with the .5-inch (1 cm) bit. Remove the tire valve's cap. Pull the valve through the hole in the PVC cap until it is firmly in place.

Make a line around the 60-inch (152 cm) PVC pipe 11 inches (28 cm) from one end. Light a candle and spin the PVC pipe over it along the line until it softens a little bit. Push the two ends together so the soft part bulges out a little. Let the pipe cool and harden.

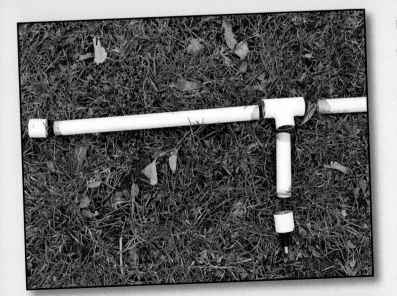

Use PVC cement as you connect each piece. First, connect the 12-inch (30 cm) PVC pipe to the tee. Then connect the 60-inch (152 cm) PVC pipe to the other side of the tee. Connect the 3-inch (8 cm) PVC pipe to the open joint of the tee and put the cap with the valve onto the open end. Put the second cap on the open end of the 12-inch (30 cm) PVC pipe.

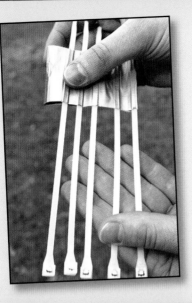

On a 3-inch (8 cm) strip of duct tape, evenly space five or six cable ties so that they face the same direction and their square heads line up evenly. Make sure the heads all face up. Put another piece of duct tape over the untaped side of the ties.

Slide a 2-liter bottle onto the 60-inch (152 cm) PVC pipe so that it rests against the bulge. Place the taped cable ties against the PVC pipe so that the square heads catch the lip of the bottle. Secure the hose clamp around the duct tape. Remove the bottle.

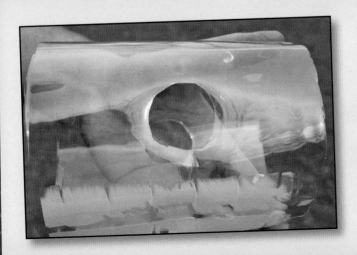

Take a 2-liter bottle and cut off its top and bottom. Hold the 2-inch (5 cm) length of PVC pipe against the bottle and use the inside of the pipe to trace a circle. Cut out the circle you just drew. Cut a slightly smaller circle out on the other side of the bottle.

Slide the cut bottle over the PVC pipe and cable ties so that it rests against the clamp. Tie your rope around the 2-inch (5 cm) length of PVC pipe. Slide the PVC pipe over the end of the 60-inch (152 cm) PVC pipe and feed its rope through the holes in the 2-liter bottle.

Fill a 2-liter bottle about a third of the way up with water. Lean the launcher down and pull on the rope. Slide the bottle onto the PVC pipe, and then release the rope. The 2-inch (5 cm) PVC pipe will slide up over the ties and rest against the bottle.

Now all you have to do is launch your water rocket. Point the launcher straight into the air and attach the bicycle tire pump to the tire valve. Add up to 50 pounds per square inch of pressure, but not more because the pipes could break. When you're ready, pull the string and watch the bottle shoot high into the sky!

Super High-Tech Projects!

Catapults and water rockets are only the beginning. The Internet is full of high-tech flying object projects for you to try! The next paragraphs describe some of them. Links to each can be found in the Projects Links box on the following page.

Rockets can go pretty fast and far when they shoot straight up. However, remote-controlled planes can go in all kinds of directions.

This hovercraft has a camera on it. Many people put cameras on their flying machines so they can take breathtaking pictures and videos.

Makezine has a video series that teaches you everything you need to know to make a remote-controlled (RC) plane. You could even go one step further and make an unmanned aerial vehicle, or UAV.

One amazing project to try is the Brain-Controlled RC Helicopter. It takes a lot of parts and you'll need an adult's help, but being able to show this project off is definitely worth it.

Projects Links

RC Plane - Makezine.com/makerhangar
UAV - Copter.ardupilot.com/wiki/introduction
Brain Copter - Instructables.com/id/Brain-Controlled-RC-Helicopter

Keep Making!

Making flying objects can be tricky at first. The more you make, though, the easier it'll become. When you build something yourself, you learn a lot about the science that makes it work. This will help you make projects that are even more exciting.

Making your own flying machine is a big accomplishment. Each time you make a new one, try to make it go higher, farther, or faster.

There are websites where people share their projects. Ask an adult to help you post pictures of your projects on one of them.

Building flying objects is just one way to get involved in the maker movement. Look at sites like Makezine.com and Instructables.com for all sorts of amazing high-tech DIY projects. Try building a robot, making a musical instrument, or programming a **microcontroller**! Once you start making, you will never want to stop!

It is best to use your flying objects in a large open space. If something goes wrong and the flying object crashes, it won't hurt anyone or anything.

More About Making

The lists below will show you more ways to learn about all kinds of flying object projects. You can also ask an adult to help you use the library and search the Internet for other projects, books, and stores!

Books

Austin, John. *Mini Weapons of Mass Destruction: Build Implements of Spitball Warfare*. Chicago: Chicago Review Press, 2009.

Baldwin, Breck. *DIY RC Airplanes from Scratch*. New York: McGraw Hill/TAB Electronics, 2013.

Harper, Gavin. *50 Model Rocket Projects for the Evil Genius*. New York: McGraw Hill/Tab Electronics, 2006.

Magazines

Electric Flight
Make

Websites

- Find parts and kits for rockets, RC airplanes, and more at Estesrockets.com.
- Learn how to build all kinds of catapults at Stormthecastle.com /catapult.index.htm.
- Learn about, buy parts for, and find instructions to build UAVs at Diydrones.org.

Glossary

catapults (KA-tuh-pults) Machines that are able to throw heavy objects.

engines (EN-jinz) Machines inside of things that make them move.

fuel (FYOO-el) Something burned to make energy, warmth, or power.

fulcrum (FUL-krum) The point on which a lever pivots.

gunpowder (GUN-pow-dur) An explosive powder.

igniter (ig-NYT-ur) A device used to start something from a distance.

medieval (meh-DEE-vul) Having to do with the Middle Ages, the years from AD 500 to AD 1450.

microcontroller (MY-kroh-kun-troh-lur) A small computer embedded in an electronic device.

propel (pruh-PEL) To move forward with force.

satellites (SA-tih-lyts) Machines in space that circle Earth to gather information.

Index

Websites

Due to the changing nature of Internet links, PowerKids Press has developed an online list of websites related to the subject of this book. This site is updated regularly. Please use this link to access the list: www.powerkidslinks.com/maker/fly/